Trip to Ireland

QUILTS COMBINING TWO OLD FAVORITES

Elizabeth Hamby Carlson

Martingale™
& COMPANY

Acknowledgments

Many thanks to:

Mary Green, Dawn Anderson, Darra Williamson, and all the staff at Martingale & Company for their help and enthusiasm;

Dolores Pilla, who not only made stars for "Irish Stars" but has been a wonderful source of encouragement every step of the way;

Jean Jarrard for encouraging words and crisis management on several occasions;

Leah Richard, machine quilter extraordinaire, for letting me jump the queue so the quilts would be ready on time;

My husband, Ken, who helps in any way that he can and puts up with a lot so I can do these things; and

All my Irish Trip quilt students, who helped improve the patterns with their ideas and suggestions, and—by their enthusiasm—inspired me to write this book.

Credits

President . . . . Nancy J. Martin
CEO . . . . Daniel J. Martin
Publisher . . . . Jane Hamada
Editorial Director . . . . Mary V. Green
Managing Editor . . . . Tina Cook
Technical Editor . . . . Darra Williamson
Copy Editor . . . . Ellen Balstad
Design Director . . . . Stan Green
Illustrator . . . . Laurel Strand
Cover and Text Designer . . . . Jennifer LaRock Shontz
Photographer . . . . Brent Kane

That Patchwork Place® is an imprint of Martingale & Company™.

Trip to Ireland: Quilts Combining Two Old Favorites
© 2002 by Elizabeth Hamby Carlson

Martingale & Company
20205 144th Avenue NE
Woodinville, WA 98072-8478 USA
www.martingale-pub.com

Printed in Hong Kong
07 06 05 04 03 02   8 7 6 5 4 3 2 1

Mission Statement

We are dedicated to providing quality products and service by working together to inspire creativity and to enrich the lives we touch.

Library of Congress Cataloging-in-Publication Data

Carlson, Elizabeth Hamby.
   Trip to Ireland : quilts combining two old favorites /
   Elizabeth Hamby Carlson.
      p. cm.
   Includes bibliographical references.
   ISBN 1-56477-417-1
      1. Patchwork—Patterns. 2. Quilting—Patterns.
      3. Appliqué—Patterns. I. Title.

TT835 .C3735 2003
746.46'041—dc21

2001057949

Contents

Introduction

The simple and traditional Irish Chain has long been my favorite pieced pattern. More than twenty-five years ago, I was already admiring old Irish Chain quilts and thinking about making one. However, the thought of cutting and sewing all those squares together—by hand!—stopped me cold. It would be boring, and I knew I would never stick to the task. Then, with the invention of the rotary cutter, quilt-making changed forever. The resulting efficient quick-cutting and piecing methods suddenly made this pattern seem much more accessible.

In the last twenty years, I have made Irish Chain quilts of every size and description: single, double, and triple chains; and chains combined with other patterns, both pieced and occasionally appliquéd.

The quilts in this book combine the Irish Chain pattern with another old favorite pattern, Trip around the World. All of the quilts, which I refer to as Irish Trip quilts, are fun to plan and fun to make.

My first Irish Trip quilt was "1776! Irish Trip in Miniature"—a red, white, and blue miniature. I thought I would start small to get the kinks worked out, which was not a brilliant plan on my part. As I well knew but chose to ignore, miniatures present their own challenges! Despite a few difficulties, however, I managed to finish the miniature, and then I couldn't wait to make a full-size version. I've been making and teaching how to make Irish Trip quilts ever since.

Irish Trip quilt classes are always exciting and stimulating sessions. Bolts of fabric are stacked everywhere as we hunt for just the right fabrics for each student's quilt. A cooperative atmosphere prevails, and we all learn from the shared experience. Until now I have been able to share my Irish Trip quilts with only a relatively small

"1776! Irish Trip in Miniature"
by Elizabeth Hamby Carlson, 30" x 30".
Bold chains in rich, patriotic colors stand in high contrast to the light background fabrics, yielding a visually strong and highly graphic pattern in this miniature version of an Irish Trip quilt. The strips were cut 1" wide and trimmed after sewing to reduce bulk. Please note that this quilt, which is not recommended for beginners, is shown for inspiration only; no directions are provided in the book.

number of people who can take my classes. However, with this book—*Trip to Ireland*—I can share these quilts with a worldwide community of quiltmakers. I am very grateful to Martingale & Company for making it possible. To all my fellow quilters, I wish you a wonderful "trip to Ireland"!

How to Use This Book

The basic construction methods used to make these quilts vary little from project to project, so techniques and tips for cutting, sewing, and pressing are summarized in "General Directions," beginning below. You will also find guidance in selecting fabrics and directions for making a fabric mock-up of your quilt pattern, which makes cutting and sewing the actual quilt go more smoothly.

Please read the "General Directions" carefully before beginning your quilt, and refer to them as needed.

In the quilt projects, beginning on page 19, step-by-step instructions include yardage, cutting, and sewing specifics for three different variations of each project. For example, "Quick and Easy Irish Trip" on page 19 offers a choice of a set of fifteen, thirty-five, or sixty-three blocks. Additionally, you can select from two different-sized strips for each project, with color-coded yardage and cutting charts to help you identify the appropriate information quickly.

Once again, I urge you to read through the complete step-by-step directions before you begin a specific project. The measurements have been checked for accuracy, but always measure your own work, particularly before cutting borders.

General Directions

Choosing Fabric

One of the things I love best about the Irish Trip designs is their versatility. Depending upon the fabrics you choose, your quilt can be as soft as a pastel watercolor, as bold as a Navajo blanket, or fall anywhere in between. You might base your fabric selection on the room where you will use your quilt, or perhaps draw inspiration from a gorgeous print fabric.

You also have a great deal of flexibility in determining the number of fabrics you choose to use in the pattern. An Irish Trip quilt can include up to fourteen different fabrics, or far fewer if you repeat the same fabric in various positions throughout the quilt.

Fabrics for these strip-pieced quilts must be chosen carefully, as once cut, different areas of the fabric's printed design will appear at random in the finished quilt. Fabrics with overall, "every which way" printed motifs are more suitable than fabrics with strong one-way or linear designs. Pattern scale and density are also important considerations. For example, large, widely spaced motifs may look spotty when strip-pieced.

An easy way to begin selecting fabric is to choose a multicolored theme or palette fabric that features colors you like. Fabrics that go well with the palette fabric will generally work well together in your quilt. A palette fabric can be used as the background fabric or to establish key areas of the basic pattern. It can also be used to tie the entire design together, by repeating in the quilt's border.

6

A lovely and light Smithsonian reproduction floral (bottom right) set the style and mood for "Smithsonian Irish Trip" (page 24). I used this print for both the background and the borders, and then I relied on its various colors to select the remaining fabrics.

Subtle tone-on-tone prints, with differing values of a single color, are ideal for mixing with—and toning down—busier multicolored printed fabrics. Because they tend to "read" as solids, tone-on-tones allow the eye a place to rest. Tone-on-tone prints, particularly neutrals such as cream, beige, and white, make a good alternate choice as background fabrics for your quilt.

For the best results, strive for a mix of multicolored and subtle tone-on-tone prints in your quilt.

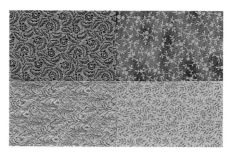

Examples of subtle tone-on-tone prints

Emphasizing Design Elements

As you choose fabrics, you'll also want to consider the main design elements in the pattern you've chosen. Some projects have two main design elements: the chain and the trip around the world.

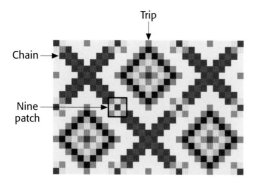

The contrast (or lack of contrast) created by placement of color and value determines which design elements will be strongest, so you'll need to decide in advance which elements you wish to emphasize. Chain fabrics with low contrast to the background, coupled with high-contrast trip fabrics, make the trip the dominant element, and vice versa. Neither element dominates when similar value and color contrast are used for both the chain **and** the trips.

Pay special attention to contrast when secondary design elements interrupt the main chain. In "Smithsonian Irish Trip" (page 24), as in the illustration at left, a third design element (the nine-patch) interrupts the chain. In "Crossing Chains" (detail below), a secondary chain crosses the main chain, connecting the trips. The value of the fabric in the corners and centers of the nine-patch, or the inner fabric of the crossing chain, should be similar to that of the inner fabric of the main chain. If it is much lighter, or much darker, the main chain will be visually broken.

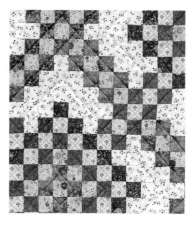

"Crossing Chains" detail. The light blue center of the main chain is very close in value to the yellow in the center of the crossing chain. For a full view of this quilt, see page 31.

Making a Mock-Up

Before you begin your project, take time to make a fabric mock-up of a section of the finished quilt. My Irish Trip quilt students all begin with this step and invariably tell me what an enormous help it is.

A mock-up not only familiarizes you with the pattern, but it also helps you select fabric and predetermine its placement. You will be able to tell from the mock-up how your fabrics will look once they have been cut into strips and segments, and reassembled into blocks for your quilt. Often I find myself shifting fabrics from one position to another, eliminating some fabrics and adding others, until I am satisfied that the finished project fulfills my expectations. I consider this preparation a minimal investment when compared to the time and fabric involved in making a complete, full-sized quilt! Follow these steps to make a fabric mock-up:

1. Draw a grid of 1" squares on a large sheet of graph paper. The grid should be at least 2 blocks wide by 1 block plus several rows long, so it is large enough for you to see the overall pattern.
2. Clearly mark the strip-set numbers along the top of the grid. Identify each square in the grid with its fabric position letter as shown. You'll find this identification information in the step-by-step instructions for each specific project.

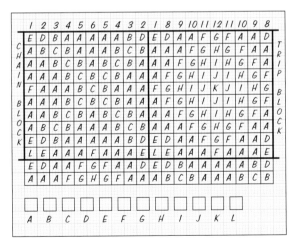

3. Use your rotary cutter to cut a 1" strip of each fabric you'll be using in your quilt. (I use the leftover strip that results from straightening the edge of each fabric.) Cut each strip into 1" squares.

4. Referring to the block diagram(s) provided in your quilt's instructions, use a temporary gluestick to attach the fabric squares to the grid on your graph paper.
5. When you have settled on the final fabric arrangement, use the gluestick and leftover squares to make a fabric key that is clearly labeled at the bottom of the grid.

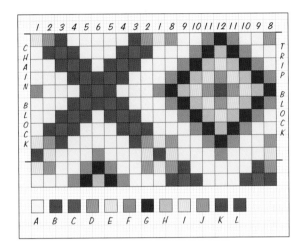

Cutting Straight Strips

Follow these steps for perfectly straight strips every time! Directions are for cutting right-handed; reverse the directions if you are left-handed.

1. Fold and press the fabric so the selvages meet. Smooth the fabric so there are no wrinkles, pulls, or puckers.
2. Place the folded fabric on the cutting board with the fold closest to you. Align the bottom edge of a small rotary ruler or quilter's square with the folded edge of the fabric. Place another ruler alongside the left edge of the first ruler.

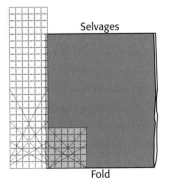

Selvages

Fold

8

3. Remove the first (small) ruler and use your rotary cutter to straighten the fabric's left edge.

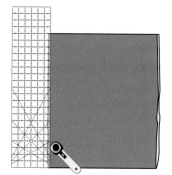

4. Fold the fabric a second time, and place it on your cutting mat with the new fold nearest you. Use your rotary ruler to make certain the 2 folds are exactly parallel to each other. This is very important: for the strips to be straight, the folds must be parallel, and the newly trimmed edge must be perpendicular (at a perfect right angle) to both folds.

5. Repeat steps 2 and 3 to retrim the fabric edge. You are now cutting 4 layers at once.

6. Align the newly cut edge of the fabric with the ruler markings for the desired strip width. Cut a strip, and open it to check that it is straight. Continue cutting strips as needed, checking periodically to be sure strips are still straight. If not, repeat the steps for folding and aligning fabric.

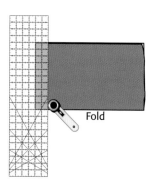

Fold

Use the grid lines on your cutting mat for alignment only. Never use them for measuring. Always measure with your ruler.

Sewing Accurate Seams

The success of your quilt depends on sewing accurate and consistent ¼"-wide seams. Use a scrap of ¼" graph paper or the ¼" marking on your rotary ruler to measure a seam guide on the throatplate of your sewing machine. Layer a few 1" strips of masking tape to mark the spot.

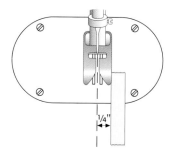

To check the accuracy of your seam guide, cut three 1½" x 6" test strips: two dark and one light. Sew a light and dark strip together; then measure the distance from one raw edge to the seam line: it should measure exactly 1¼". Press the seam toward the darker fabric.

Sew the second dark strip to the remaining long raw edge of the lighter strip in the previously sewn pair. Press the new seam away from the light strip. If the seam allowances are accurate, the center strip will now measure 1". If not, try again!

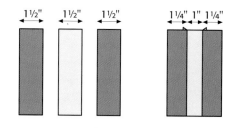

Making Strip Sets

Sewn and pressed strip sets should be even, flat, and straight. The more strips in a set, the more the tendency for the unit to curve, resulting in the dreaded bowed strip set.

Half-length strip sets are made exactly like full-length sets, but with 42"-long strips that are first divided into two strips, each 21" long. The individual project instructions indicate how many full-length strips to cut and, with a number in parentheses, how many to divide into shorter strips for half-length strip sets.

Sewing

1. Place 2 adjacent strips right sides together, aligning the top and the long raw edges, and pinning if necessary. Sew the strips together from top to bottom, stopping periodically (with the needle down) to realign the raw edges as needed. Do not pull on the strips as you sew; allow the machine's feed dogs to move the fabric along. Sew the remaining pairs of strips for the set and press seams as indicated in the project instructions, and as described in "Pressing" at right.

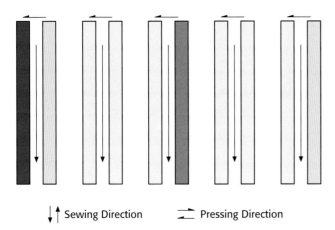

↓↑ Sewing Direction   ⇄ Pressing Direction

2. Align the top edges of 2 sewn and pressed pairs of strips. Pin them to secure, and then reverse the sewing direction from step 1, stitching them from bottom to top. Join the remaining pressed pairs to complete the strip set.

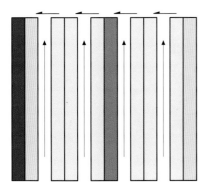

3. Use a safety pin to identify the top corner of the first strip in each completed set.

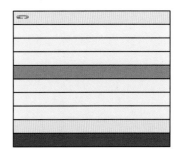

Pressing

Set your iron to the cotton setting. (I use steam for a good, firm press.) Carefully follow the pressing arrows provided with each project so that seam allowances will oppose, or nest, when blocks and rows are sewn together.

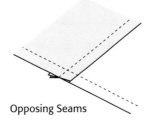

Opposing Seams

Generally, all seams in each strip set are pressed in one direction: toward either the first or the last strip in the set.

> Always press each seam before sewing additional strips to a set. Never sew a strip to an unpressed set!

Tips for Staying Organized

While cutting and sewing these projects is easy, keeping track of all the strips and strip sets can be a bit confusing, particularly for those quilts with large, asymmetrical blocks. Follow these simple tips for organizing, and the job will go smoothly.

◆ Keep your mock-up in clear view and refer to it as you work. I pin mine to my design wall, and refer to it often as I make the strip sets and blocks.

◆ Organize cut strips in the order in which they will be sewn, and label them by letter. The latter step is especially helpful when you are repeating a particular fabric in more than one lettered position in the blocks. A fold-up rack for drying clothes makes a great strip and strip-set organizer. You can place the cut strips, and later the strip sets, on the wooden rods, where they hang neatly and don't clutter your work surface.

◆ Use the chain-piecing method when sewing strip sets. Lay the strips for one set to the left of your sewing machine, with the first strip in the set nearest the machine. Sew the first and second strips together. Then—without clipping the thread—chain sew the remaining pairs (such as the third and fourth strips, fifth and sixth strips, etc.) in the set. This method keeps all pairs of strips for one set together.

Strips for a single strip set, organized for sewing

◆ If you are making multiple identical strip sets, stack the strips for as many sets as you need. Sew the first and second strips together for all identical sets; then sew the third and fourth strips together, and so on.

Crosscutting Strip Sets

Once strip sets are sewn and pressed, you'll need to crosscut them into segments. You may crosscut strip sets one at a time, or layer them and cut two at once. Always place cut segments so the first fabric in the segment is at the top, and label stacks of segments with their strip-set number. Remember: accuracy and organization count!

Crosscutting Strip Sets Singly

1. Place a strip set wrong side up on your cutting mat. Align the horizontal lines on a small rotary ruler or quilter's square so they are parallel to the seam lines on the sewn strip set. Refer to "Cutting Straight Strips," steps 2 and 3 on pages 7–8, and trim the left edge of the strip set.

2. Align the newly cut edge of the strip set with the ruler markings for the desired segment width. Double-check that the horizontal lines on the ruler are still parallel to the seam lines of the strip set. Crosscut the desired number of segments.

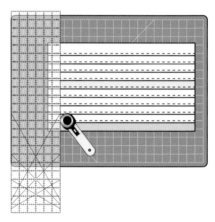

Crosscutting Strip Sets in Layers

Layering and cutting paired strip sets is a real time-saver, and a good way to check for accuracy. Try it once you've become confident with your cutting skills.

Using the Chain block from "Smithsonian Irish Trip" on page 11 as an example, note that a segment from strip set 2 is consistently sewn to a segment from strip set 3, and a segment from strip set 4 is consistently sewn to one from strip set 5.

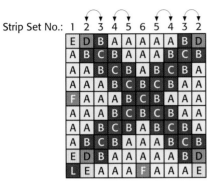

Strip Set No.: 1 2 3 4 5 6 5 4 3 2

Identify the paired strips in each block.

These paired strip sets can be layered right sides together on the cutting mat, and crosscut together. Pairs of cut segments are ready to pick up and sew, with their long raw edges already aligned for stitching. Like pairs can be chain-pieced, saving a great deal of time. When you study the block diagrams for each project, identify these paired segments in each block.

Follow these steps for cutting layered pairs of strip sets. For purposes of illustration, we'll pair strip set 2 with strip set 3 in the instructions.

1. Place strip set 2 on the mat, right side up. The safety pin in the first strip should be in the top left corner.

2. Place strip set 3 on top of strip set 2, right sides together, with the bottom end of strip set 3 aligned with the top end of strip set 2. (This reversal is necessary because many of these strip sets are asymmetrical.) The safety pin in the first strip of strip set 3 should be in the top right corner. Pull back the top left corner of strip set 3 and double-check the strip's placement against your mock-up. If the strip

sets have been sewn and pressed correctly, the seam allowances of the sets should nest together perfectly.

3. Refer to "Crosscutting Strip Sets Singly," steps 1 and 2 on page 10, to straighten the edges and to crosscut the strip-set pair into segments. Do not separate the pairs of segments; they are ready to sew together.

> Use the side of your ruler to gently shift the cut pairs of segments. I cut on a large mat on my cutting table, and then I use the ruler to transfer the pairs to a small mat I can carry to my machine.

Sewing the Blocks

Block diagrams indicating sewing order are included in the instructions for each project. Just as with strip sets, it is easiest to sew segments in pairs first, and then join the pairs.

Strip Set No.: 1 2 3 4 5 6 5 4 3 2

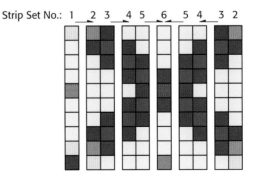

Block Assembly Diagram

12

When joining layered pairs, note that like pairs are not all sewn on the same edge. For example, each block will have a segment from strip set 2 sewn to a segment from strip set 3 for the left side of the block, and a segment from strip set 3 sewn to a segment from strip set 2 for the right side of the block. Keep this in mind when assembling the blocks.

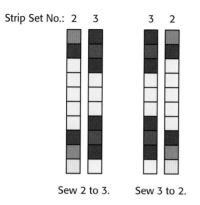

Strip Set No.: 2   3   3   2

Sew 2 to 3.   Sew 3 to 2.

It is usually unnecessary to pin the segments for sewing; the nested seam allowances help keep things in place. Use a stiletto or small screwdriver to guide the segments under the presser foot and to adjust or ease as needed. Sew the segments together from seam to seam, pausing (with the needle down) after crossing each seam to assure the next seam is aligned properly. Press each seam before adding another segment to the block.

Adding Borders

Whenever possible, I like to wait until the center of the quilt is complete before making a final decision on borders. This allows me to audition various fabrics and/or fabric combinations for maximum flexibility.

Border measurements are given for each quilt plan, but since variations in size can occur during quilt construction, always measure your own work before cutting borders.

Straight-Cut Borders

For quilts with multiple straight-cut borders, add the inner border to all four sides first, and then add the outer borders one at a time, in the same sequence.

1. Measure the length of the quilt top through its center. Cut side borders of the required width to match this measurement. Use a pin to mark the center of each border strip and the center of each side of the quilt. Pin the borders to the quilt top, matching the center points and outer edges; then stitch. Press the seam allowances toward the borders.

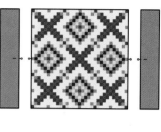

2. Measure the width of the quilt through its center, including the side borders you've just added. Cut top and bottom borders of the required width to match this measurement. Pin and sew the top and bottom borders to the quilt top as described in step 1. Press the seam allowances toward the borders.

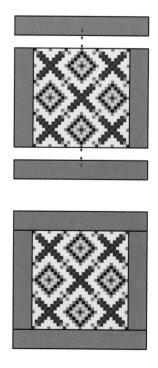

Mitered Borders

Mitered borders are especially effective when you are using striped fabrics (see "Irish Stars" on page 43), or adding multiple borders. Cut strips for a mitered border the full length or width of the quilt—including borders—plus an extra inch. When the quilt has more than one border to be mitered, cut all border strips for each side the same length as the outermost border, and sew the strips together to create a single border unit.

I sew mitered corners closed with an invisible hand stitch. This method allows me to work from the right side of the quilt, and I find it to be nearly foolproof, especially for multiple or striped borders.

1. Measure the quilt through its vertical center. To this measurement, add twice the width of the borders, plus 1". Cut 2 border strips of the desired width to this length for side borders.

2. Measure the quilt through its horizontal center, and repeat step 1 to cut 2 border strips of the desired width to this length for top and bottom borders.

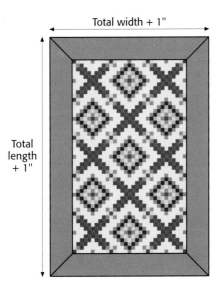

Total width + 1"

Total length + 1"

3. Use a pin to mark the center of each border strip and the center of each side of the quilt top. On each border strip, also measure and mark one-half the length (or width) of the quilt top from each side of the center pin.

4. Place a border strip and the quilt top right sides together, matching the center points. Also match the outer pins to the raw edges of the quilt top. Sew the border strip to the quilt, beginning and ending with a backstitch ¼" from the corners of the quilt top. Press the seam toward the border. Repeat on each side of the quilt.

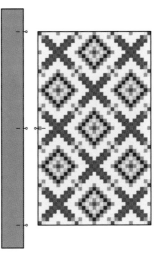

5. Lay the quilt on an ironing board so the top border extends over the side borders. Fold under one corner of the top border at a 45° angle, using the 45° marking on your ruler as a guide. Press the fold and pin it securely by placing pins perpendicular to the fold.

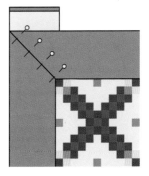

6. Working from the right side, carefully hand sew the mitered corner closed with tiny, invisible hand stitches. Repeat this process for the remaining 3 corners, trimming the seams to ¼" and pressing them open.

Layering and Basting

Choice of batting often depends on your quilting plan. For machine-quilted quilts, I prefer a light- to medium-weight cotton batting. The quilt shrinks up just a bit when it is washed, giving the quilt a vintage look. For hand quilting, I prefer polyester batting because it is much easier for me to needle. Whichever fiber you choose, use a good-quality batting. Cut the batting approximately 3" larger than the top on all sides.

Choose backing fabric that complements the front of the quilt and the binding. The back should measure approximately 4" larger than the top on all sides. If necessary, seam the backing by dividing it crosswise (selvage to selvage), removing the selvages, and then sewing it down the middle or in three sections. Press the seams open.

Place the backing wrong side up on a clean, flat surface. Center and smooth the batting, and then the quilt top (right side up), over the backing. Baste through all the layers, beginning in the center and working out in each direction; smooth the layers as you go. For hand quilting, baste a 4" grid pattern and finish with a line of stitching all around the outside edge. For machine quilting, baste and secure the layers with safety pins.

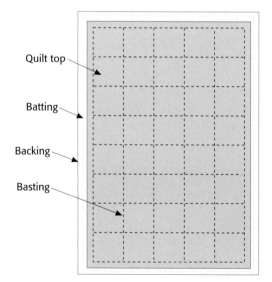

Quilt top

Batting

Backing

Basting

Quilting

Your quilt can be quilted any way you like. Most of my quilts were machine quilted.

For machine quilting, straight lines or continuous line patterns are neat and easy. Use an even-feed, or walking, foot on your machine so the layers move through the feed dogs evenly. Set your machine at eight to ten stitches per inch, and remove the safety pins as you sew. Allover quilting patterns are also very effective. Install a darning-foot attachment and drop the feed dogs to accomplish this free-motion stitching.

For more elaborate quilting patterns, such as feathers or cables, mark the top before the quilt is layered and basted. If your quilting plan features simple outline or straight-line quilting, you can mark as you go. Always test your marking tool to be sure the marks can be removed.

Hand quilting is a lovely option for a special quilt. Most quilters prefer to hand quilt in a hoop or a frame. Begin quilting in the center of the quilt, and work out in each direction to avoid puckers and bumps.

Binding

Instructions for all projects in this book include yardage required for bias binding. A walking foot will help keep the layers from shifting as you stitch the binding in place.

1. Use a rotary cutter to trim the backing and batting even with the edges of the quilt top, and to square the quilt corners. Baste the 3 layers together all around the edge to prevent shifting as you apply the binding.

2. Total the outside dimensions of the quilt (the perimeter) and add 9". Cut enough 2½"-wide bias strips from the binding fabric to equal this measurement. Join the strips with diagonal seams. Trim the seam allowances to ¼", and press them open.

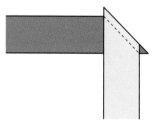

3. Trim one end of the long strip at a 45° angle, and turn under a ¼" hem. Fold the binding in half lengthwise, wrong sides together, and press.

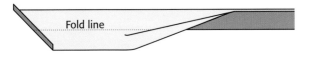

Fold line

4. Lay the binding on the front of the quilt, aligning all raw edges. Place the end of the binding approximately 10" from a corner. Begin stitching 4" from the end of the binding, taking a ⅜" seam allowance. Stop stitching ⅜" from the first corner and backstitch.

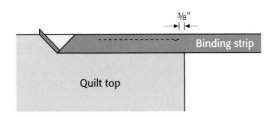

⅜"

Binding strip

Quilt top

5. Fold the binding diagonally so that it is perpendicular to the edge you just stitched. Refold the binding straight down so the corner fold is even with the edge of the quilt. Start sewing at the folded edge, beginning with a backstitch, and continue stitching around the remaining edges and corners until you are 4" from the starting point.

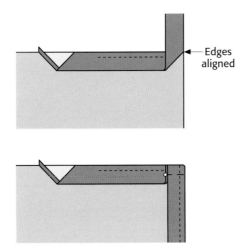

Edges aligned

6. Trim the end of the binding so it overlaps the beginning by 3". Tuck the cut end of the binding strip inside the diagonal fold. Be sure that the join is smooth on the long folded edge. Pin and finish sewing the binding to the quilt.

7. Fold the binding over the edge of the quilt and hand stitch it to the backing with an invisible hand stitch. As you fold each corner back, a miter will form on the front. To make a similar miter on the back, fold down one side of the binding and then the other. Finish the binding by hand, stitching the diagonal folds of the miters and the diagonal seam where the binding ends.

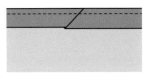

Quilt Gallery

"Irish Trip" by Elizabeth Hamby Carlson, 77" x 77". Quilted by Lizzie Borntrager.
Predominantly pink, blue, and green prints give this quilt its feminine air. The chain fabrics are
repeated in the trip, with the blue print repeated in two rings for extra emphasis.

**"Irish Trip" by Dolores Pilla,
78" x 78". Quilted by Pat Burns.**
A beautiful rose floral fabric inspired this lovely quilt. Such a busy background might pose a challenge, but Dolores obviously managed it skillfully. By selecting chain and trip fabrics in colors drawn from this print but covering a wide variety of values and scales, she has not let the background overwhelm the pieced pattern.

**"Christmas Crossing Chains"
by Elizabeth Hamby Carlson, 61" x 73".
Quilted by Pat Burns.**
Traditional Christmas colors make this a cozy winter quilt. Three different background fabrics—all neutrals but in varying values—give this quilt its distinctive look.

"Irish Trip" by Melanie Westerfeld, 80" x 101". Quilted by Leah Richard.
Melanie used Moda's Morning Glory fabric collection, designed by Robyn Pandolph, to make this soft and lovely quilt. The low-contrast, floral trip fabrics create a watercolor effect, while the chain's less-patterned fabrics with slightly higher contrast suggest a path between the flower beds of a beautiful garden.

"Irish Trip"
by Nancy McDonald, 78" x 78".
Nancy made her flower-filled quilt as a going-away-to-college gift for her daughter. The high-contrast, periwinkle fabric emphasizes the inner chain. A multicolor pansy print appears in two rings of the trip and is repeated in the outer border. Nancy hand-quilted her charming quilt—a special present indeed!

Quick and Easy Irish Trip

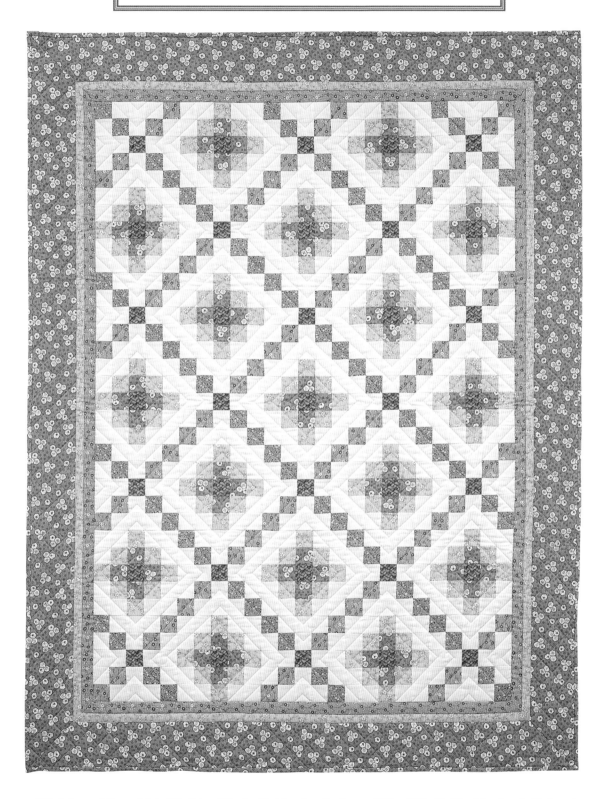

"Quick and Easy Irish Trip" by Elizabeth Hamby Carlson, 51" x 66". Quilted by Leah Richard.

Cheerful '30s reproduction fabrics lend a sunny look to this simple yet charming quilt for a child.

Perfect for beginners, this easy-to-stitch, cheerful quilt goes together quickly. Make one just for fun or as a warm-up to the other projects in this book. Select a strip width and follow the appropriate color-coded charts. The quilt diagram on page 23 indicates the block setting plans (3 x 5, 5 x 7, and 7 x 9) to make quilts in various sizes.

FINISHED BLOCK SIZES

STRIP WIDTH	BLOCK SIZE
2"	7½"
2½"	10"

FINISHED QUILT SIZES

STRIP WIDTH	3 x 5 BLOCKS	5 x 7 BLOCKS	7 x 9 BLOCKS
2"	35½" x 50½"	50½" x 65½"	65½" x 80½"
2½"	43" x 63"	63" x 83"	83" x 103"

MATERIALS: 42"-WIDE FABRIC

STRIP WIDTH	3 x 5 BLOCKS	5 x 7 BLOCKS	7 x 9 BLOCKS
Fabric A (white subtle print for background)			
2"	⅞ yd.	1⅝ yds.	3⅛ yds.
2½"	1⅛ yds.	2⅞ yds.	4 yds.
Fabric B (blue print for chain)			
2"	¼ yd.	⅜ yd.	½ yd.
2½"	¼ yd.	½ yd.	¾ yd.
Fabric C (green print for chain)			
2"	¼ yd.	⅜ yd.	½ yd.
2½"	¼ yd.	½ yd.	¾ yd.
Fabric D (red print for chain and trip)			
2"	⅛ yd.	¼ yd.	⅜ yd.
2½"	⅛ yd.	⅜ yd.	⅜ yd.
Fabric E (yellow print for trip)			
2"	⅜ yd.	⅝ yd.	1 yd.
2½"	⅜ yd.	⅞ yd.	1¼ yds.
Fabric F (blue print for trip)			
2"	¼ yd.	⅜ yd.	⅝ yd.
2½"	¼ yd.	½ yd.	¾ yd.
*Green print for inner border**			
2"	¼ yd.	⅜ yd.	½ yd.
2½"	⅜ yd.	⅜ yd.	½ yd.
*Yellow print for middle border***			
2"	¼ yd.	⅜ yd.	⅜ yd.
2½"	⅜ yd.	⅜ yd.	½ yd.
*Blue print for outer border****			
2"	1½ yds.	2 yds.	2½ yds.
2½"	1⅞ yds.	2½ yds.	3 yds.

STRIP WIDTH	3 x 5 BLOCKS	5 x 7 BLOCKS	7 x 9 BLOCKS
*Blue print for binding****			
2"	⅔ yd.	¾ yd.	⅞ yd.
2½"	⅔ yd.	⅞ yd.	1 yd.
Backing			
2"	1⅝ yds.	4 yds.	4⅞ yds.
2½"	3⅞ yds.	5 yds.	6⅛ yds.
Batting			
2"	42" x 56"	56" x 72"	72" x 87"
2½"	49" x 70"	70" x 89"	89" x 109"

*I used the same green print as fabric C. If you plan to repeat a fabric in more than one position, add the yardages for each position together.

**I used the same yellow print as fabric E.

***I used the same blue print as fabric F.

Cutting the Strips for Strip Sets and Borders

Refer to the cutting charts on page 21. Cut the required number of strips in the appropriate width to make the quilt size you have chosen. Cut all strips across the full width of the fabric (selvage to selvage) unless directed otherwise. All cut measurements include ¼"-wide seam allowances. Numbers in parentheses indicate how many full strips to cut in half for half-length strip sets. Refer to "Cutting Straight Strips" (page 7) for additional guidance as needed.

NUMBER OF STRIPS FOR STRIP SETS

FABRIC	STRIP WIDTH	NUMBER OF STRIPS		
		3 x 5 BLOCKS	5 x 7 BLOCKS	7 x 9 BLOCKS
A	2"	14 (8)	28	53 (3)
	2½"	14 (8)	39 (11)	56
B	2"	2 (2)	4	8
	2½"	2 (2)	6 (2)	8
C	2"	2 (2)	4	8
	2½"	2 (2)	6 (2)	8
D	2"	1 (1)	2	4
	2½"	1 (1)	3 (1)	4
E	2"	4 (1)	8	15
	2½"	4 (1)	11 (3)	16
F	2"	2 (1)	4	8 (1)
	2½"	2 (1)	6 (2)	8

NUMBER AND WIDTH OF BORDER STRIPS

Cut the inner and middle border strips across the width of the fabric. Cut the outer border strips along the length of the fabric.

FABRIC	STRIP WIDTH USED	NUMBER OF 1½"-WIDE INNER BORDER STRIPS		
		3 x 5 BLOCKS	5 x 7 BLOCKS	7 x 9 BLOCKS
Green print	2"	5	6	8
	2½"	6	7	9

FABRIC	STRIP WIDTH USED	NUMBER OF 1¼"-WIDE MIDDLE BORDER STRIPS		
		3 x 5 BLOCKS	5 x 7 BLOCKS	7 x 9 BLOCKS
Yellow print	2"	5	6	8
	2½"	6	7	9

FABRIC	STRIP WIDTH USED	NUMBER OF 4¾"-WIDE OUTER BORDER STRIPS		
		3 x 5 BLOCKS	5 x 7 BLOCKS	7 x 9 BLOCKS
Blue print	2"	4	4	4
	2½"	4	4	4

Making the Strip Sets

Refer to the strip set diagrams on page 22 and sew the appropriately sized and colored strips into strip sets. The strip set chart below indicates the required number of each strip set for the quilt size you are making. Press seams in odd-numbered sets toward the last strip in the set. Press seams in even-numbered sets toward the first strip in the set. Use the 21"-long strips to construct half-length strip sets. Refer to "Making Strip Sets" (page 8) as needed.

◆ **NOTE:** You may have some half strips left over.

NUMBER OF STRIP SETS

STRIP SET NUMBER	STRIP WIDTH USED	NUMBER OF STRIP SETS		
		3 x 5 BLOCKS	5 x 7 BLOCKS	7 x 9 BLOCKS
1	2"	½	1	2
	2½"	½	1, ½	2
2	2"	½	1	2
	2½"	½	1, ½	2
3	2"	½	1	2
	2½"	½	1, ½	2
4	2"	½	1	2
	2½"	½	1, ½	2
5	2"	½	1	2
	2½"	½	1, ½	2
6	2"	1	2	3, ½
	2½"	1	2, ½	4
7	2"	1	2	3, ½
	2½"	1	2, ½	4
8	2"	½	1	2
	2½"	½	1, ½	2

22

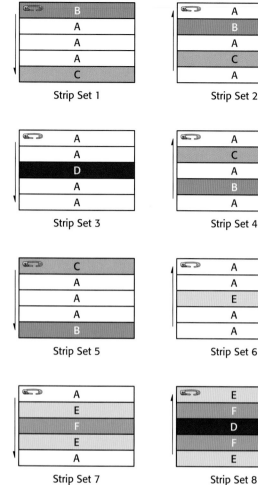

Strip Set 1

Strip Set 2

Strip Set 3

Strip Set 4

Strip Set 5

Strip Set 6

Strip Set 7

Strip Set 8

NUMBER OF SEGMENTS

STRIP SET NUMBER	NUMBER OF SEGMENTS		
	3 x 5 BLOCKS	5 x 7 BLOCKS	7 x 9 BLOCKS
1	8	18	32
2	8	18	32
3	8	18	32
4	8	18	32
5	8	18	32
6	14	34	62
7	14	34	62
8	7	17	31

Block Construction

Refer to the block diagrams below to sew the segments into the appropriate number of Chain and Trip blocks for the quilt size you are making. Press seams toward the center of the Chain blocks and away from the center of the Trip blocks. Mark the top left corner of each block with a safety pin. Refer to "Sewing the Blocks" (page 11) for guidance as needed.

Strip Set No.: 1 2 3 4 5

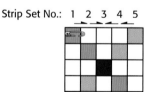

Chain Block
Make 8 for 3 x 5 block quilt.
Make 18 for 5 x 7 block quilt.
Make 32 for 7 x 9 block quilt.

Strip Set No.: 6 7 8 7 6

Trip Block
Make 7 for 3 x 5 block quilt.
Make 17 for 5 x 7 block quilt.
Make 31 for 7 x 9 block quilt.

Cutting the Segments

Refer to the segment chart at right to crosscut strip sets into the required number of segments for the quilt size you are making. Cut the segments to the same width as the individual strips in the strip sets. For example, if you are working with 2"-wide strips, cut segments 2" wide from the strip set. Keep track of the cut segments from each strip set, always placing them so the first fabric in the segment is at the top. Refer to "Crosscutting Strip Sets" (page 10) for guidance as needed. Note that the number of segments to cut in the segment chart applies to both strip widths.

Assembling the Quilt Top

1. Refer to the quilt diagram below to arrange alternating Chain and Trip blocks. Sew the blocks together in horizontal rows. Press seams toward the Chain blocks.

2. Carefully pin the rows together to match the seams; then sew the rows together. Press seams toward the bottom edge of the quilt.

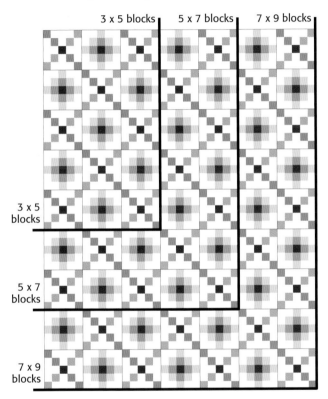

3 x 5 blocks   5 x 7 blocks   7 x 9 blocks

3 x 5 blocks

5 x 7 blocks

7 x 9 blocks

Quilt Diagram

Adding Borders

Refer to "Mitered Borders" (page 13) as needed.

1. Sew the 1½"-wide green-print strips end to end to make one continuous 1½"-wide inner border strip. Repeat with the 1¼"-wide yellow-print strips and the 4¾"-wide blue-print strips to make continuous middle and outer border strips.

2. Refer to the quilt photo on page 19 to sew the inner, middle, and outer border strips together to make a border unit. Press seams toward the middle border.

3. Measure, trim, pin, and sew the border units to the sides, top, and bottom edges of the quilt. Press seams toward the border. Miter the corners; press.

Finishing

Refer to "Layering and Basting" (page 14), "Quilting" (page 14), and "Binding" (page 14) as needed.

1. Piece the quilt backing if necessary. Center the quilt top and batting over the backing; baste.

2. Quilt as desired.

3. Trim the backing and batting. Cut the binding fabric into 2½"-wide bias strips. Sew the binding to the quilt.

"Smithsonian Irish Trip" by Elizabeth Hamby Carlson, 77" x 77". Quilted by George Anna Lunking.
Elizabeth's first full-size Irish Trip quilt was inspired by the Smithsonian
reproduction fabric used for the quilt's background and border.

Two old favorites, Irish Chain and Trip around the World, combine with little nine patches to create a simple yet versatile design. Make your quilt any way you like, from old-fashioned to brightly contemporary. Select a strip width and follow the appropriate color-coded charts. The quilt diagram on page 29 indicates the block setting plans (4 x 5, 5 x 5, and 5 x 7) to make quilts in various sizes.

FINISHED BLOCK SIZES

STRIP WIDTH	BLOCK SIZE
1¾"	12½"
2"	15"

FINISHED QUILT SIZES

STRIP WIDTH	4 x 5 BLOCKS	5 x 5 BLOCKS	5 x 7 BLOCKS
1¾"	65¾" x 78¼"	78¾" x 78¾"	78¾" x 103¾"
2"	76½" x 91½"	91½" x 91½"	91½" x 121½"

MATERIALS: 42"-WIDE FABRIC

STRIP WIDTH	4 x 5 BLOCKS	5 x 5 BLOCKS	5 x 7 BLOCKS
Fabric A (light floral print for background)			
1¾"	2¼ yds.	3¼ yds.	4¼ yds.
2"	2¾ yds.	3¾ yds.	4⅝ yds.
Fabric B (brown print for outer chain)			
1¾"	⅞ yd.	1¼ yds.	1¼ yds.
2"	1 yd.	1⅜ yds.	1¾ yds.
Fabric C (pink print for inner chain)			
1¾"	½ yd.	⅝ yd.	¾ yd.
2"	½ yd.	¾ yd.	⅞ yd.
Fabric D (medium dark blue print for nine patches)			
1¾"	¼ yd.	⅜ yd.	½ yd.
2"	⅜ yd.	½ yd.	⅝ yd.
Fabric E (light pink print for nine patches)			
1¾"	¼ yd.	⅜ yd.	½ yd.
2"	⅜ yd.	½ yd.	⅝ yd.
Fabric F (light blue print for trip)			
1¾"	⅞ yd.	⅞ yd.	1⅛ yds.
2"	⅞ yd.	1 yd.	1¼ yds.
Fabric G (dark blue print for trip)			
1¾"	⅝ yd.	¾ yd.	⅞ yd.
2"	⅞ yd.	1 yd.	1 yd.
Fabric H (tan print for trip)			
1¾"	½ yd.	⅝ yd.	¾ yd.
2"	½ yd.	¾ yd.	¾ yd.
Fabric I (light pink print for trip)			
1¾"	⅜ yd.	½ yd.	½ yd.
2"	⅜ yd.	½ yd.	½ yd.

STRIP WIDTH	4 x 5 BLOCKS	5 x 5 BLOCKS	5 x 7 BLOCKS
Fabric J (dark pink print for trip)			
1¾"	¼ yd.	¼ yd.	¼ yd.
2"	¼ yd.	⅜ yd.	⅜ yd.
Fabric K (dark red print for trip)			
1¾"	⅛ yd.	⅛ yd.	⅛ yd.
2"	⅛ yd.	⅛ yd.	⅛ yd.
Fabric L (dark red print for nine patches)			
1¾"	⅛ yd.	¼ yd.	¼ yd.
2"	⅛ yd.	¼ yd.	¼ yd.
Pink print for inner border			
1¾"	¼ yd.	⅜ yd.	½ yd.
2"	⅜ yd.	½ yd.	½ yd.
Light floral print for outer border*			
1¾"	2 yds.	2¼ yds.	2⅝ yds.
2"	2¼ yds.	2⅝ yds.	3⅛ yds.
Binding*			
1¾"	⅞ yd.	⅞ yd.	⅞ yd.
2"	⅞ yd.	⅞ yd.	1 yd.
Backing			
1¾"	4⅝ yds.	4⅝ yds.	6 yds.
2"	5⅜ yds.	8 yds.	10½ yds.
Batting			
1¾"	72" x 85"	85" x 85"	85" x 110"
2"	83" x 98"	98" x 98"	98" x 128"

*I used the same light floral print as fabric A. If you plan to repeat a fabric in more than one position, add the yardages for each position together.

Cutting the Strips for Strip Sets and Borders

Refer to the cutting charts below. Cut the required number of strips in the appropriate width to make the quilt size you have chosen. Cut all strips across the full width of the fabric (selvage to selvage) unless directed otherwise. All cut measurements include ¼"-wide seam allowances. Numbers in parentheses indicate how many full strips to cut in half for half-length strip sets. Refer to "Cutting Straight Strips" (page 7) for additional guidance as needed.

NUMBER OF STRIPS FOR STRIP SETS

FABRIC	STRIP WIDTH	NUMBER OF STRIPS		
		4 x 5 BLOCKS	5 x 5 BLOCKS	5 x 7 BLOCKS
A	1¾"	43	62 (19)	80
	2"	43	62 (19)	80
B	1¾"	15	22 (7)	28
	2"	15	22 (7)	28
C	1¾"	7	10 (3)	13
	2"	7	10 (3)	13
D	1¾"	4	6 (2)	8
	2"	4	6 (2)	8
E	1¾"	4	6 (2)	8
	2"	4	6 (2)	8
F	1¾"	10	15 (5)	20
	2"	10	16 (5)	20
G	1¾"	9	13 (4)	16
	2"	9	13 (4)	16
H	1¾"	7	10 (3)	12
	2"	7	10 (3)	12
I	1¾"	5	7 (2)	8
	2"	5	7 (2)	8
J	1¾"	3	4 (1)	4
	2"	3	4 (1)	4
K	1¾"	1	1	1
	2"	1	1	1
L	1¾"	1	2 (1)	2
	2"	1	2 (1)	2

NUMBER AND WIDTH OF BORDER STRIPS

The numbers in parentheses indicate the widths to cut the inner border strips. Cut each inner border strip across the full width of the fabric. Cut outer border strips along the length of the fabric.

FABRIC	STRIP WIDTH USED	NUMBER & WIDTH OF INNER BORDER STRIPS		
		4 x 5 BLOCKS	5 x 5 BLOCKS	5 x 7 BLOCKS
Pink print	2"	6 (1¼")	7 (1½")	8 (1½")
	2½"	7 (1½")	8 (1½")	9 (1½")

FABRIC	STRIP WIDTH USED	NUMBER OF 6½"-WIDE OUTER BORDER STRIPS		
		4 x 5 BLOCKS	5 x 5 BLOCKS	5 x 7 BLOCKS
Light floral print	2"	4	4	4
	2½"	4	4	4

Making the Strip Sets

Refer to the strip set diagrams on page 27 and sew the appropriately sized and colored strips into strip sets. The strip set chart on page 27 indicates the required number of each strip set for the quilt size you are making. Press seams in odd-numbered sets toward the last strip in the set. Press seams in even-numbered sets toward the first strip in the set. (There is no strip set 7.) Use the 21"-long strips to construct half-length strip sets. Refer to "Making Strip Sets" (page 8) for guidance as needed.

◆ **NOTE:** You may have some half strips left over.

NUMBER OF STRIP SETS

STRIP SET NUMBER	STRIP WIDTH USED	NUMBER OF STRIP SETS		
		4 x 5 BLOCKS	5 x 5 BLOCKS	5 x 7 BLOCKS
1	1¾"	1	1, ½	2
	2"	1	1, ½	2
2	1¾"	1	1, ½	2
	2"	1	1, ½	2
3	1¾"	1	1, ½	2
	2"	1	1, ½	2
4	1¾"	1	1, ½	2
	2"	1	1, ½	2
5	1¾"	1	1, ½	2
	2"	1	1, ½	2
6	1¾"	1	1	1
	2"	1	1	1
8*	1¾"	1	1, ½	2
	2"	1	1, ½	2
9	1¾"	1	1, ½	2
	2"	1	1, ½	2
10	1¾"	1	1, ½	2
	2"	1	1, ½	2
11	1¾"	1	1, ½	2
	2"	1	1, ½	2
12	1¾"	1	1	1
	2"	1	1	1

*There is no strip set 7.

Cutting the Segments

Refer to the segment chart below to crosscut strip sets into the required number of segments for the quilt size you are making. Cut the segments to the same width as the individual strips in the strip sets. For example, if you are working with 2"-wide strips, cut segments 2" wide from the strip sets. Keep track of the cut segments from each strip set, placing them so the first fabric in the segment is at the top. Refer to "Crosscutting Strip Sets" (page 10) for guidance. Note that the number of segments to cut in the segment chart is for both strip widths.

NUMBER OF SEGMENTS

STRIP SET NUMBER	NUMBER OF SEGMENTS		
	4 x 5 BLOCKS	5 x 5 BLOCKS	5 x 7 BLOCKS
1	21	26	36
2	20	26	36
3	20	26	36
4	20	26	36
5	20	26	36
6	13	13	18
8	20	24	34
9	20	24	34
10	20	24	34
11	20	24	34
12	12	12	17

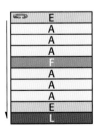

Strip Set 1

Strip Set 2

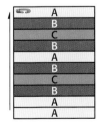

Strip Set 3

Strip Set 4

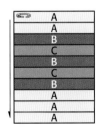

Strip Set 5

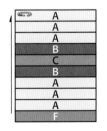

Strip Set 6

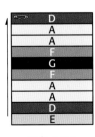

Strip Set 8

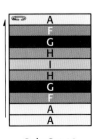

Strip Set 9

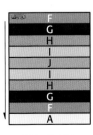

Strip Set 10

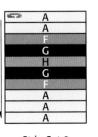

Strip Set 11

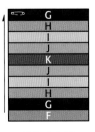

Strip Set 12

Block Construction

Refer to the block diagrams below to sew the segments into the appropriate number of Chain and Trip blocks (and half blocks, if you are making the 4 x 5 block set). Press seams toward the center of the Chain blocks and away from the center of the Trip blocks. Mark the top left corner of each block with a safety pin. Refer to "Sewing the Blocks" (page 11) for guidance as needed.

Strip
Set No.:   1 2 3 4 5 6 5 4 3 2

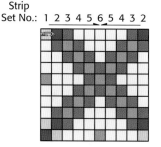

1 8 9 10 11 12 11 10 9 8

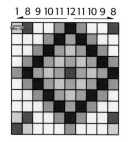

Chain Block
Make 7 for 4 x 5 block quilt.
Make 13 for 5 x 5 block quilt.
Make 18 for 5 x 7 block quilt.

Trip Block
Make 8 for 4 x 5 block quilt.
Make 12 for 5 x 5 block quilt.
Make 17 for 5 x 7 block quilt.

Strip Set No.:   6 5 4 3 2

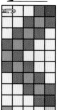

1 2 3 4 5 6

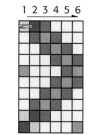

Left-Half Chain Block
Make 3 for
4 x 5 block quilt.

Right-Half Chain Block
Make 3 for
4 x 5 block quilt.

Strip Set No.:   12 11 10 9 8

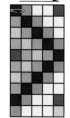

1 8 9 10 11 12

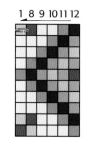

Left-Half Trip Block
Make 2 for
4 x 5 block quilt.

Right-Half Trip Block
Make 2 for
4 x 5 block quilt.

Assembling the Quilt Top

1. Refer to the row diagrams below to arrange alternating Chain and Trip blocks (and half blocks, if you are making the 4 x 5 block set). Sew the blocks together into horizontal rows. Press seams toward the Chain blocks.

   If you are making a 5 x 5 or 5 x 7 block set, cut and add a segment from strip set 1 to the right edge of each row as shown. Press.

Strip Set 1

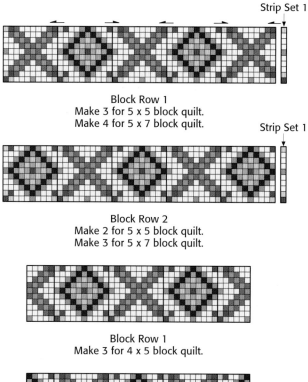

Block Row 1
Make 3 for 5 x 5 block quilt.
Make 4 for 5 x 7 block quilt.

Strip Set 1

Block Row 2
Make 2 for 5 x 5 block quilt.
Make 3 for 5 x 7 block quilt.

Block Row 1
Make 3 for 4 x 5 block quilt.

Block Row 2
Make 2 for 4 x 5 block quilt.

2. To make the quilt top symmetrical, an extra row must be added to the top edge of the quilt. This row must be sewn separately so the grain line matches the rest of the quilt. Using the diagram on page 29 as a guide, cut the required number of squares of each fabric. The measurement of each square should equal the strip width for the quilt you are making.

Lay out the row with the lengthwise grain of each square running top to bottom (parallel to the side edges of the quilt top). Sew the squares together, and press as illustrated.

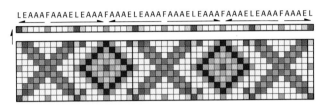

For 5 x 5 block and 5 x 7 block quilts, sew this extra row to top edge of first row of blocks.

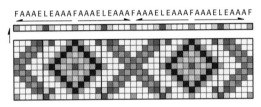

For 4 x 5 block quilt, sew this extra row to top edge of first row of blocks.

3. Refer to the quilt diagram at right. Beginning with the row from step 2, lay out the quilt center by alternating rows from step 1. Carefully pin the rows together to match the seams; then sew the rows together. Press the seams toward the bottom edge of the quilt.

Adding Borders

Refer to "Straight-Cut Borders" (page 12) as needed.

1. Sew the 42"-long pink-print inner border strips end to end to make one continuous inner border strip. Measure, trim, pin, and sew the inner border strips to the sides, top, and bottom edges of the quilt. Press seams toward the border.

2. Measure, trim, pin, and sew a 6½"-wide, light floral-print, outer border strip to the sides, top, and bottom edges of the quilt. Press seams toward the outer border.

Finishing

Refer to "Layering and Basting" (page 14), "Quilting" (page 14), and "Binding" (page 14) as needed.

1. Piece the quilt backing if necessary. Center the quilt top and batting over the backing; baste.

2. Quilt as desired.

3. Trim the backing and batting. Cut the binding fabric into 2½"-wide bias strips. Sew the binding to the quilt.

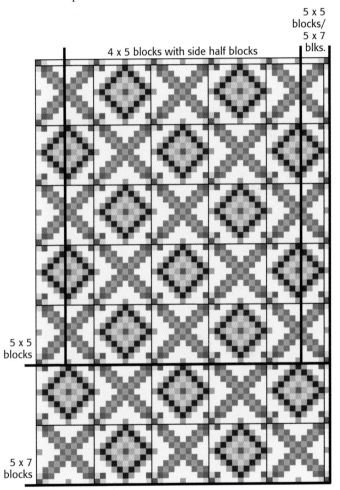

Quilt Diagram

Baby Irish Trip

**"Baby Irish Trip" by Elizabeth Hamby Carlson,
43¾" x 51¼". Quilted by Lorraine Carter.**

The "Smithsonian Irish Trip" pattern makes a wonderful baby quilt. In this 4-block-by-5-block version, the finished block measures 7½". Strips for all strip sets are cut 1¼" wide.

To make a baby-sized version of this classic pattern, you'll need the following materials:

- 1⅝ yds. fabric A
- ⅝ yd. fabric B
- ½ yd. each fabrics C, F, G, H, and binding
- ¼ yd. each fabrics D, E, I, J, K, L, and inner border
- 1¼ yds. outer border
- 3½ yds. backing
- 50" x 61" piece batting

Cut the following strips. Cut each strip 1¼" by the full width of the fabric, unless directed otherwise.

- 43 strips fabric A
- 15 strips fabric B
- 7 strips fabric C
- 4 strips each fabrics D and E
- 10 strips fabric F
- 9 strips fabric G
- 7 strips fabric H
- 5 strips fabric I
- 3 strips fabric J
- 1 strip each fabrics K and L
- 4 strips, each 1" by width of fabric, inner border
- 4 strips, each 6½" by **length** of fabric, outer border

Make 1 of each strip set as directed on page 26. Follow the instructions for constructing the 4-block-by-5-block version of "Smithsonian Irish Trip" (pages 27–29).

Crossing Chains

"Crossing Chains" by Elizabeth Hamby Carlson, 63" x 78". Quilted by Leah Richard.
This quilt, a variation of the basic Irish Trip quilt, has a second chain that crosses the main chain and connects the trips. Lively blues, greens, and yellows lend a Dutch country flavor to this quilt.

This variation of the Irish Trip quilt features an additional chain that connects the Trip blocks. Select a strip size and follow the appropriate color-coded charts. The quilt diagram on page 36 indicates the block setting plans (4 x 5, 5 x 5, and 5 x 7) to make quilts in various sizes.

FINISHED BLOCK SIZES

STRIP WIDTH	BLOCK SIZE
1¾"	12½"
2"	15"

FINISHED QUILT SIZES

STRIP WIDTH	4 x 5 BLOCKS	5 x 5 BLOCKS	5 x 7 BLOCKS
1¾"	66¼" x 78¾"	78¾" x 78¾"	78¾" x 103¾"
2"	76½" x 91½"	91½" x 91½"	91½" x 121½"

MATERIALS: 42"-WIDE FABRIC

STRIP WIDTH	4 x 5 BLOCKS	5 x 5 BLOCKS	5 x 7 BLOCKS
Fabric A (light floral print for background)			
1¾"	2¼ yds.	2¾ yds.	3⅝ yds.
2"	2½ yds.	3¼ yds.	4 yds.
Fabric B (green print for outer chain)			
1¾"	⅞ yd.	1¼ yds.	1½ yds.
2"	1 yd.	1⅜ yds.	1⅝ yds.
Fabric C (light blue print for inner chain)			
1¾"	½ yd.	¾ yd.	⅞ yd.
2"	⅝ yd.	⅞ yd.	1 yd.
Fabric D (medium dark blue-print for crossing chain)			
1¾"	½ yd.	¾ yd.	⅞ yd.
2"	⅝ yd.	¾ yd.	1 yd.
Fabric E (yellow print 1 for crossing chain)			
1¾"	⅜ yd.	⅜ yd.	½ yd.
2"	⅜ yd.	½ yd.	⅝ yd.
Fabric F (dark blue print for trip)			
1¾"	⅝ yd.	⅞ yd.	1⅛ yds.
2"	¾ yd.	1 yd.	1¼ yds.
Fabric G (yellow print 2 for trip)			
1¾"	½ yd.	¾ yd.	⅞ yd.
2"	⅝ yd.	⅞ yd.	1 yd.
Fabric H (medium blue print for trip)			
1¾"	½ yd.	⅝ yd.	¾ yd.
2"	½ yd.	¾ yd.	¾ yd.
Fabric I (light blue print for trip)			
1¾"	⅜ yd.	½ yd.	½ yd.
2"	⅜ yd.	½ yd.	⅜ yd.

STRIP WIDTH	4 x 5 BLOCKS	5 x 5 BLOCKS	5 x 7 BLOCKS
Fabric J (dark green print for trip)			
1¾"	¼ yd.	⅜ yd.	⅜ yd.
2"	¼ yd.	⅜ yd.	⅜ yd.
Fabric K (light blue print for trip)			
1¾"	⅛ yd.	⅛ yd.	⅛ yd.
2"	¼ yd.	¼ yd.	¼ yd.
Fabric L (yellow print for trip)			
1¾"	⅛ yd.	¼ yd.	¼ yd.
2"	¼ yd.	¼ yd.	¼ yd.
Green print for inner and outer border*			
1¾"	2¼ yds.	2¼ yds.	3 yds.
2"	2⅝ yds.	2⅝ yds.	3½ yds.
Light blue print for middle border**			
1¾"	½ yd.	½ yd.	½ yd.
2"	½ yd.	½ yd.	⅝ yd.
Binding*			
1¾"	⅞ yd.	⅞ yd.	⅞ yd.
2"	⅞ yd.	⅞ yd.	1 yd.
Backing			
1¾"	4⅝ yds.	4⅝ yds.	6 yds.
2"	5⅜ yds.	8 yds.	10½ yds.
Batting			
1¾"	73" x 85"	85" x 85"	85" x 110"
2"	83" x 98"	98" x 98"	98" x 128"

*I used the same green print as fabric B. If you plan to repeat a fabric in more than one position, add the yardages for each position together.

**I used the same light blue print as fabric C.

Cutting the Strips for Strip Sets and Borders

Refer to the cutting charts below. Cut the required number of strips in the appropriate width to make the quilt size you have chosen. Cut all strips across the full width of the fabric (selvage to selvage) unless directed otherwise. All cut measurements include ¼"-wide seam allowances. Numbers in parentheses indicate how many full strips to cut in half for half-length strip sets. Refer to "Cutting Straight Strips" (page 7) for additional guidance as needed.

NUMBER OF STRIPS FOR STRIP SETS

FABRIC	STRIP WIDTH	NUMBER OF STRIPS		
		4 x 5 BLOCKS	5 x 5 BLOCKS	5 x 7 BLOCKS
A	1¾"	37	53 (16)	68
	2"	37	53 (16)	68
B	1¾"	15	22 (7)	28
	2"	15	22 (7)	28
C	1¾"	9	13 (4)	17
	2"	9	13 (4)	17
D	1¾"	8	12 (4)	16
	2"	8	12 (4)	16
E	1¾"	4	6 (2)	8
	2"	4	6 (2)	8
F	1¾"	11	16 (5)	20
	2"	11	16 (5)	20
G	1¾"	9	13 (4)	16
	2"	9	13 (4)	16
H	1¾"	7	10 (3)	12
	2"	7	10 (3)	12
I	1¾"	5	7 (2)	8
	2"	5	7 (2)	8
J	1¾"	3	4 (1)	4
	2"	3	4 (1)	4
K	1¾"	1	1	1
	2"	1	1	1
L	1¾"	1	2 (1)	2
	2"	1	2 (1)	2

NUMBER AND WIDTH OF BORDER STRIPS

Cut the inner and middle border strips across the width of the fabric. Cut the outer border strips along the length of the fabric.

FABRIC	STRIP WIDTH USED	NUMBER OF 2"-WIDE INNER BORDER STRIPS		
		4 x 5 BLOCKS	5 x 5 BLOCKS	5 x 7 BLOCKS
Green print	1¾"	4	4	4
	2"	4	4	4

FABRIC	STRIP WIDTH USED	NUMBER OF 1½"-WIDE MIDDLE BORDER STRIPS		
		4 x 5 BLOCKS	5 x 5 BLOCKS	5 x 7 BLOCKS
Light blue print	1¾"	6	8	9
	2"	9	9	11

FABRIC	STRIP WIDTH USED	NUMBER OF 5"-WIDE OUTER BORDER STRIPS		
		4 x 5 BLOCKS	5 x 5 BLOCKS	5 x 7 BLOCKS
Green print	1¾"	4	4	4
	2"	4	4	4

Making the Strip Sets

Refer to the strip set diagrams on page 34 and sew the appropriately sized and colored strips into strip sets. The strip set chart on page 34 indicates the required number of each strip set for the quilt size you are making. Press seams in odd-numbered sets toward the last strip in the set. Press seams in even-numbered sets toward the first strip in the set. (There is no strip set 7.) Use the 21"-long strips to construct half-length strip sets. Refer to "Making Strip Sets" (page 8) as needed.

◆ **NOTE:** You may have some half strips left over.

NUMBER OF STRIP SETS

STRIP SET NUMBER	STRIP WIDTH USED	NUMBER OF STRIP SETS		
		4 x 5 BLOCKS	5 x 5 BLOCKS	5 x 7 BLOCKS
1	1¾"	1	1, ½	2
	2"	1	1, ½	2
2	1¾"	1	1, ½	2
	2"	1	1, ½	2
3	1¾"	1	1, ½	2
	2"	1	1, ½	2
4	1¾"	1	1, ½	2
	2"	1	1, ½	2
5	1¾"	1	1, ½	2
	2"	1	1, ½	2
6	1¾"	1	1	1
	2"	1	1	1
8*	1¾"	1	1, ½	2
	2"	1	1, ½	2
9	1¾"	1	1, ½	2
	2"	1	1, ½	2
10	1¾"	1	1, ½	2
	2"	1	1, ½	2
11	1¾"	1	1, ½	2
	2"	1	1, ½	2
12	1¾"	1	1	1
	2"	1	1	1

*There is no strip set 7.

Cutting the Segments

Refer to the segment chart below to crosscut strip sets into the required number of segments for the quilt size you are making. Cut the segments to the same width as the individual strips in the strip sets. For example, if you are working with 2"-wide strips, cut the segments 2" wide from the strip set. Keep track of the cut segments from each strip set, always placing them so the first fabric in the segment is at the top. Refer to "Crosscutting Strip Sets" (page 10) for guidance as needed. Note that the number of segments to cut in the segment chart is for both strip widths.

NUMBER OF SEGMENTS

STRIP SET NUMBER	NUMBER OF SEGMENTS		
	4 x 5 BLOCKS	5 x 5 BLOCKS	5 x 7 BLOCKS
1	20	25	35
2	20	26	36
3	20	26	36
4	20	26	36
5	20	26	36
6	13	13	18
8	20	24	34
9	20	24	34
10	20	24	34
11	20	24	34
12	12	12	17

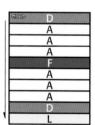

Strip Set 1

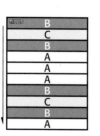

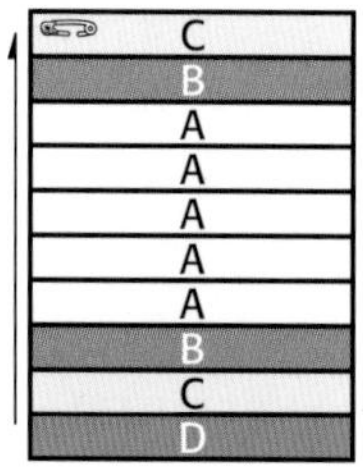

Strip Set 2

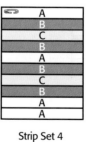

Strip Set 3

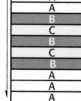

Strip Set 4

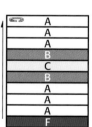

Strip Set 5

Strip Set 6

Strip Set 8

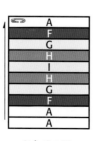

Strip Set 9

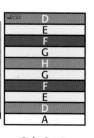

Strip Set 10

Strip Set 11

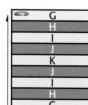

Strip Set 12

Block Construction

Refer to the block diagrams below to sew the segments into the appropriate number of Chain and Trip blocks (and half blocks, if you are making the 4 x 5 block set). Press seams toward the center of the Chain blocks and away from the center of the Trip blocks. Mark the top left corner of each block with a safety pin. Refer to "Sewing the Blocks" (page 11) for guidance as needed.

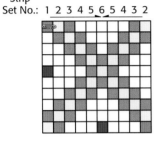

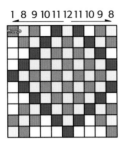

Strip
Set No.: 1 2 3 4 5 6 5 4 3 2

1 8 9 10 11 12 11 10 9 8

Chain Block
Make 7 for 4 x 5 block quilt.
Make 13 for 5 x 5 block quilt.
Make 18 for 5 x 7 block quilt.

Trip Block
Make 8 for 4 x 5 block quilt.
Make 12 for 5 x 5 block quilt.
Make 17 for 5 x 7 block quilt.

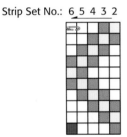

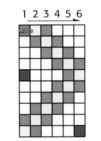

Strip Set No.: 6 5 4 3 2

1 2 3 4 5 6

Left-Half Chain Block
Make 3 for
4 x 5 block quilt.

Right-Half Chain Block
Make 3 for
4 x 5 block quilt.

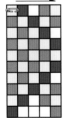

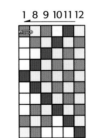

Strip Set No.: 12 11 10 9 8

1 8 9 10 11 12

Left-Half Trip Block
Make 2 for
4 x 5 block quilt.

Right-Half Trip Block
Make 2 for
4 x 5 block quilt.

Assembling the Quilt Top

1. Refer to the row diagrams below to arrange alternating Chain and Trip blocks (and half blocks, if you are making the 4 x 5 block set). Sew the blocks together into horizontal rows. Press seams toward the Chain blocks.

    If you are making a 5 x 5 or 5 x 7 block set, cut and add a segment from strip set 1 to the right edge of each row as shown. Press.

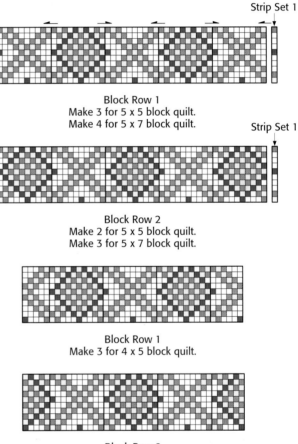

Strip Set 1

Block Row 1
Make 3 for 5 x 5 block quilt.
Make 4 for 5 x 7 block quilt.

Strip Set 1

Block Row 2
Make 2 for 5 x 5 block quilt.
Make 3 for 5 x 7 block quilt.

Block Row 1
Make 3 for 4 x 5 block quilt.

Block Row 2
Make 2 for 4 x 5 block quilt.

2. To make the quilt top symmetrical, an extra row must be added to the top edge of the quilt. This row must be sewn separately so the grain line matches the rest of the quilt. Using the diagram on page 36 as a guide, cut the required number of squares of each fabric. The measurement of each square should equal the strip width for the quilt you are making.

Lay out the row with the lengthwise grain of each square running top to bottom (parallel to the side edges of the quilt top). Sew the squares together, and press as illustrated.

For 5 x 5 block and 5 x 7 block quilts, sew this extra row to top edge of first row of blocks.

For 4 x 5 block quilt, sew this extra row to top edge of first row of blocks.

3. Refer to the quilt diagram at right. Beginning with the row from step 2, lay out the quilt center by alternating rows from step 1. Carefully pin the rows together to match the seams; then sew the rows together. Press the seams toward the bottom edge of the quilt.

Adding Borders

Refer to "Mitered Borders" (page 13) as needed.

1. Sew the 2"-wide green-print inner border strips end to end to make one continuous 2"-wide inner border strip. Repeat with the 1½"-wide light blue-print middle border strips and the 5"-wide green-print outer border strips to make continuous middle and outer border strips.

2. Refer to the quilt photo on page 32 to sew the inner, middle, and outer border strips together to make a border unit. Press seams toward the middle border.

3. Measure, trim, pin, and sew the border unit to the sides, top, and bottom edges of the quilt. Press seams toward the border unit. Miter the corners; press.

Finishing

Refer to "Layering and Basting" (page 14), "Quilting" (page 14), and "Binding" (page 14) as needed.

1. Piece the quilt backing if necessary. Center the quilt top and batting over the backing; baste.

2. Quilt as desired.

3. Trim the backing and batting. Cut the binding fabric into 2½"-wide bias strips. Sew the binding to the quilt.

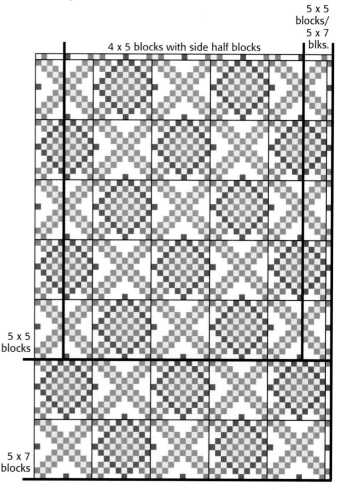

Quilt Diagram

Irish Squares

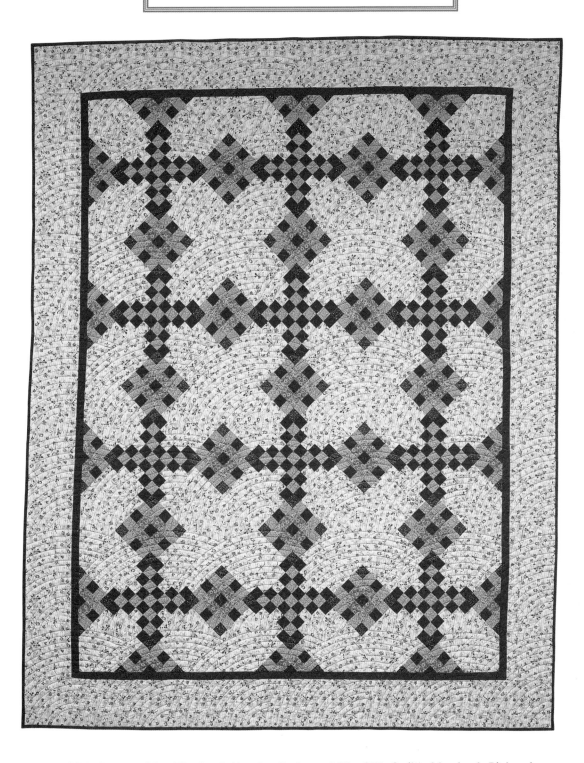

"Irish Squares" by Elizabeth Hamby Carlson, 68" x 85". Quilted by Leah Richard.
An on-point set, with its strong diagonal lines, gives the basic Irish Chain
pattern a fresh, new look and a strong masculine flavor.

S etting the blocks on point runs the chain in this quilt vertically and horizontally rather than diagonally. Five patches interrupt—but don't quite break—the chains, adding another design element. Select a strip width and follow the appropriate color-coded charts. The quilt diagram on page 42 indicates the block setting plans (3 x 3, 3 x 4, and 4 x 5) to make quilts in various sizes.

FINISHED BLOCK SIZES

STRIP WIDTH	BLOCK SIZE
1¾"	12½"
2"	15"

FINISHED QUILT SIZES

STRIP WIDTH	3 x 3 BLOCKS	3 x 4 BLOCKS	4 x 5 BLOCKS
1¾"	67⅞" x 67⅞"	67⅞" x 85½"	85½" x 103⅛"
2"	78¾" x 78¾"	78¾" x 100"	100" x 121¼"

MATERIALS: 42"-WIDE FABRIC

STRIP WIDTH	3 x 3 BLOCKS	3 x 4 BLOCKS	4 x 5 BLOCKS
Fabric A (tan floral print for background)			
1¾"	3¼ yds.	4 yds.	5½ yds.
2"	4½ yds.	5 yds.	7 yds.
Fabric B (dark red print for chain and setting blocks)			
1¾"	1 yd.	1¼ yds.	1⅝ yds.
2"	1⅛ yds.	1½ yds.	2 yds.
Fabric C (light blue print for chain and setting blocks)			
1¾"	⅞ yd.	1⅛ yds.	1½ yds.
2"	1 yd.	1⅛ yds.	1¾ yds.
Fabric D (dark green print for chain and setting blocks)			
1¾"	⅜ yd.	½ yd.	⅝ yd.
2"	½ yd.	½ yd.	¾ yd.
Fabric E (light green print for chain and setting blocks)			
1¾"	⅜ yd.	⅜ yd.	⅝ yd.
2"	½ yd.	½ yd.	¾ yd.
Fabric F (light red print for chain and setting blocks)			
1¾"	⅜ yd.	⅜ yd.	⅝ yd.
2"	⅜ yd.	½ yd.	⅝ yd.
Dark red print for inner border*			
1¾"	⅜ yd.	⅜ yd.	½ yd.
2"	⅜ yd.	½ yd.	½ yd.
Tan floral print for outer border**			
1¾"	2 yds.	2⅛ yds.	2⅝ yds.
2"	2¼ yds.	2½ yds.	3⅛ yds.
Binding*			
1¾"	¾ yd.	⅞ yd.	⅞ yd.
2"	⅞ yd.	⅞ yd.	1 yd.

STRIP WIDTH	3 x 3 BLOCKS	3 x 4 BLOCKS	4 x 5 BLOCKS
Backing			
1¾"	4 yds.	5 yds.	9¾ yds.
2"	4¾ yds.	6 yds.	10½ yds.
Batting			
1¾"	74" x 74"	74" x 92"	92" x 110"
2"	85" x 85"	85" x 106"	106" x 128"

*I used the same dark red print as fabric B. If you plan to repeat a fabric in more than one position, add the yardages for each position together.

**I used the same tan floral print as fabric A.

Cutting the Strips for Strip Sets and Borders

Refer to the cutting charts on page 39. Cut the required number of strips in the appropriate width to make the quilt size you have chosen. Cut all strips across the full width of the fabric (selvage to selvage) unless directed otherwise. All cut measurements include ¼"-wide seam allowances. Numbers in parentheses indicate how many full strips to cut in half for half-length strip sets. Refer to "Cutting Straight Strips" (page 7) for additional guidance as needed.

NUMBER AND WIDTH OF FABRIC A STRIPS FOR STRIP SETS

This project requires fabric A strips cut in several different widths. Locate your chosen strip width in the chart (1¾" or 2"); then cut the required number of A strips listed. Label these strips by letter (A1, A2, etc.) as you cut them.

STRIP WIDTH USED	FABRIC A STRIP WIDTH	NUMBER OF STRIPS		
		3 x 3 BLOCKS	3 x 4 BLOCKS	4 x 5 BLOCKS
1¾"	1¾"—A1	2	3 (1)	4
	3"—A2	2	3 (1)	4
	4¼"—A3	3 (1)	4 (1)	5
	5½"—A4	1 (1)	1	1
	6¾"—A5	5 (1)	7 (1)	11 (1)
	13"—A7*	4	4	6
2"	2"—A1	1	2 (1)	2
	3½"—A2	2	3 (1)	4
	5"—A3	3 (1)	4 (1)	5
	6½"—A4	1 (1)	1	1
	8"—A5	7 (2)	9 (2)	11 (1)
	15½"—A7*	4	4	6

* There is no A6 strip.

NUMBER AND WIDTH OF SEGMENTS FROM FABRIC A7 STRIPS

Crosscut fabric A7 strips into segments as follows. These segments are used as strip set 7 segments.

STRIP WIDTH USED	SEGMENT WIDTH	NUMBER OF SEGMENTS		
		3 x 3 BLOCKS	3 x 4 BLOCKS	4 x 5 BLOCKS
1¾"	6¾"	16	20	30
2"	8"	16	20	30

NUMBER OF REMAINING FABRIC STRIPS FOR STRIP SETS

FABRIC	STRIP WIDTH	NUMBER OF STRIPS		
		3 x 3 BLOCKS	3 x 4 BLOCKS	4 x 5 BLOCKS
B	1¾"	17 (3)	24 (7)	30 (2)
	2"	18 (3)	25 (5)	33 (2)
C	1¾"	15 (3)	20 (3)	29
	2"	16 (2)	21 (4)	29
D	1¾"	5 (1)	7 (1)	10
	2"	6	7 (1)	10
E	1¾"	6 (2)	6 (1)	10 (1)
	2"	6 (2)	8 (1)	10 (1)
F	1¾"	5 (1)	6	10
	2"	5 (1)	7 (1)	10

NUMBER OF BORDER STRIPS

Cut all inner border strips across the width of the fabric. Cut all outer border strips along the length of the fabric.

FABRIC	STRIP WIDTH USED	NUMBER OF 1½"-WIDE INNER BORDER STRIPS		
		3 x 3 BLOCKS	3 x 4 BLOCKS	4 x 5 BLOCKS
Dark red print	1¾"	6	7	8
	2"	7	8	10

FABRIC	STRIP WIDTH USED	NUMBER OF 6½"-WIDE OUTER BORDER STRIPS		
		3 x 3 BLOCKS	3 x 4 BLOCKS	4 x 5 BLOCKS
Tan floral print	1¾"	4	4	4
	2"	4	4	4

Making the Strip Sets

Refer to the strip set diagrams below and sew the appropriately sized and colored strips into strip sets. The strip set chart indicates the required number of each strip set for the quilt size you are making. Press seams in odd-numbered sets toward the last strip in the set. Press seams in even-numbered sets toward the first strip in the set. Use the 21"-long strips to construct half-length strip sets. Refer to "Making Strip Sets" (page 8) for guidance as needed.

◆ **NOTE:** You may have some half strips left over.

NUMBER OF STRIP SETS

STRIP SET NUMBER	STRIP WIDTH USED	NUMBER OF STRIP SETS		
		3 x 3 BLOCKS	3 x 4 BLOCKS	4 x 5 BLOCKS
1	1¾"	2, ½	3	5
	2"	2, ½	3, ½	5
2	1¾"	1	1, ½	2
	2"	1	1, ½	2
3	1¾"	1	1, ½	2
	2"	1	1, ½	2
4	1¾"	1	1, ½	2
	2"	1	1, ½	2
5	1¾"	½	1	1
	2"	½	1	1
6	1¾"	1, ½	1, ½	2, ½
	2"	1, ½	2	2, ½
8	1¾"	1, ½	2	3
	2"	2	2	3

Cutting the Segments

Refer to the segment chart below to crosscut strip sets into the required number of segments for the quilt size you are making. Cut the segments to the same width as the individual strips in the strip sets. For example, if you are working with 2"-wide strips, cut the segments 2" wide from the strip set. Keep track of the cut segments from each strip set, always placing them so the first fabric in the segment is at the top. Refer to "Crosscutting Strip Sets" (page 10) for guidance as needed. Note that the number of segments to cut in the segment chart is for both strip widths.

NUMBER OF SEGMENTS

STRIP SET NUMBER	NUMBER OF SEGMENTS		
	3 x 3 BLOCKS	3 x 4 BLOCKS	4 x 5 BLOCKS
1	50	64	100
2	18	24	40
3	18	24	40
4	18	24	40
5	9	12	20
6	25	32	50
8	32	40	60

Strip Set 1

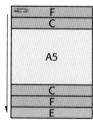

Strip Set 2

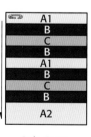

Strip Set 3

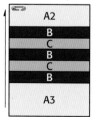

Strip Set 4

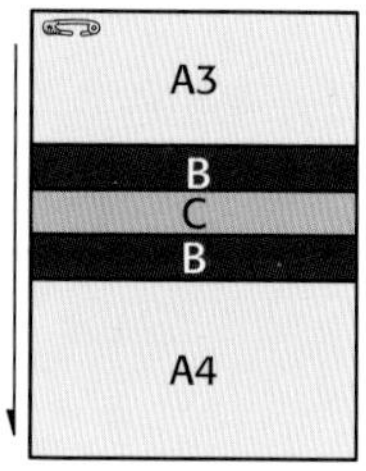

Strip Set 5

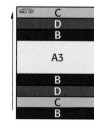

Strip Set 6

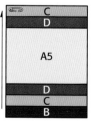

Strip Set 8

Block Construction

Refer to the block diagrams below to sew the segments into the appropriate number of Chain and setting blocks. Press seams toward the center of the Chain blocks and away from the center of the setting blocks. Mark the top right corner of each block with a safety pin. Refer to "Sewing the Blocks" (page 11) for guidance as needed.

Strip
Set No.: 1 2 3 4 5 4 3 2 1 6   1 8   7   8 1 6

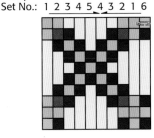 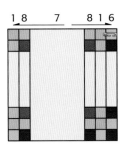

Chain Block
Make 9 for 3 x 3 block quilt.
Make 12 for 3 x 4 block quilt.
Make 20 for 4 x 5 block quilt.

Setting Block
Make 16 for 3 x 3 block quilt.
Make 20 for 3 x 4 block quilt.
Make 30 for 4 x 5 block quilt.

> Variations in sewing and pressing may result in some Chain blocks finishing smaller than they should. Measure and note the size of a representative Chain block. If necessary, trim the strip set 7 segment of the setting blocks to compensate.

Assembling the Quilt Top

1. From leftover fabric B, cut the following number of squares: 3 squares for the 3 x 3 block set, 4 squares for the 3 x 4 block set, or 5 squares for the 4 x 5 block set. Cut the squares to the same size as the basic strip width for the quilt size you are making.

2. Refer to the assembly diagram at right and the quilt diagram on page 42 to arrange diagonal rows of alternating Chain and setting blocks. Place all the blocks so the top right corner (with the safety pin) is closest to the top of the quilt. The setting blocks will extend beyond the outside edges and will be trimmed later.

3. Sew 1 square from step 1 to the bottom left corner of the setting blocks along the left edge of the quilt as shown below. Note that the final setting block does not get a square from step 1.

4. Sew the blocks together in diagonal rows. Press seams toward the Chain blocks. Carefully pin the rows together to match the seams; then sew the rows together. Press seams toward the bottom edge of the quilt.

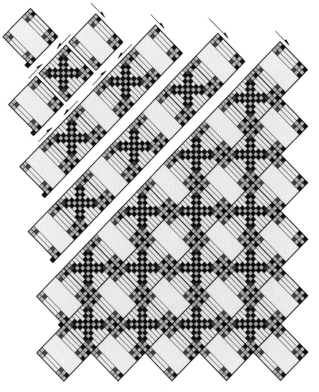

Assembly Diagram

Adding Borders

Refer to "Straight-Cut Borders" (page 12) as needed.

1. Lay the assembled quilt on a clean, flat surface. Use a pencil and ruler to mark a line around the edge of the quilt, ¼" outside the sewing line.

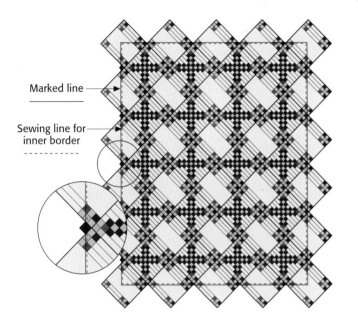

Marked line —→

Sewing line for inner border —→

2. Sew the 1½"-wide dark red strips end to end to make a continuous 1½"-wide inner border strip.

3. Measure the length of the quilt top through its center between the top and bottom lines drawn in step 1. Cut 2 inner border strips to this measurement from the 1½"-wide inner border strip. Pin the inner borders to the sides of the quilt, right sides together and aligning the raw edge of each border with the left- or right-side line drawn in step 1. Sew the borders to the quilt.

Make certain the borders are sewn properly; then use a rotary cutter to trim the excess setting blocks even with the long raw edge of the border strip. Press seams toward the border.

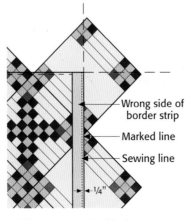

Wrong side of border strip

Marked line

Sewing line

¼"

Trim excess setting blocks.

4. Measure the width of the quilt through its center, including the borders you've just added. Cut 2 inner border strips to this measurement from the remaining 1½"-wide inner border strip from step 2. Pin the inner borders to the top and bottom of the quilt, aligning the raw edge of each border with the top or bottom line drawn in step 1. Sew the borders to the quilt; then trim the excess setting blocks. Press seams toward the border.

5. Sew the 6½"-wide tan floral outer border strips end to end to make one continuous 6½"-wide outer border strip. Measure, trim, pin, and sew the outer border to the sides, top, and bottom of the quilt; press.

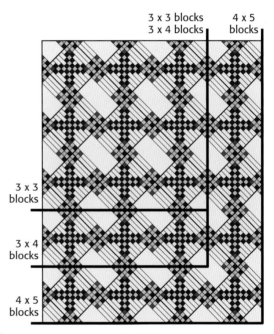

3 x 3 blocks
3 x 4 blocks

4 x 5 blocks

3 x 3 blocks

3 x 4 blocks

4 x 5 blocks

Quilt Diagram

Finishing

Refer to "Layering and Basting" (page 14), "Quilting" (page 14), and "Binding" (page 14) as needed.

1. Piece the quilt backing if necessary. Center the quilt top and batting over the backing; baste.

2. Quilt as desired.

3. Trim the backing and batting. Cut the binding fabric into 2½"-wide bias strips. Sew the binding to the quilt.

Irish Stars

"Irish Stars" by Elizabeth Hamby Carlson and Dolores Pilla, 49" x 64". Quilted by Leah Richard.
Sawtooth Stars combine with a double Irish Chain pattern in this traditional quilt, crafted from Civil War
reproduction fabrics. Different fabrics appear in each star, enhancing the quilt's old-fashioned, scrappy feel.

"Irish Stars" combines the Irish Chain with another easily constructed and well-loved pattern, the Sawtooth Star. The scrappy stars provide a good opportunity to use those enticing fabric packets all quilters seem to love! Select a strip width and follow the appropriate color-coded charts. The quilt diagram on page 47 indicates the block setting plans (3 x 5, 5 x 7, and 7 x 9) to make quilts in various sizes.

FINISHED BLOCK SIZES

STRIP WIDTH	BLOCK SIZE
2"	7½"
2½"	10"

FINISHED QUILT SIZES

STRIP WIDTH	3 x 5 BLOCKS	5 x 7 BLOCKS	7 x 9 BLOCKS
2"	33½" x 48½"	48½" x 63½"	63½" x 78½"
2½"	41" x 61"	61" x 81"	81" x 101"

MATERIALS: 42"-WIDE FABRIC

STRIP WIDTH	3 x 5 BLOCKS	5 x 7 BLOCKS	7 x 9 BLOCKS
Fabric A (blue print for inner chain)			
2"	⅜ yd.	⅝ yd.	1 yd.
2½"	½ yd.	1 yd.	1⅜ yds.
Fabric B (red print for outer chain)			
2"	⅝ yd.	1 yd.	1¾ yds.
2½"	¾ yd.	1⅝ yds.	2⅜ yds.
Fabric C (subtle neutral print for background)			
2"	¾ yd.	1⅜ yds.	2¼ yds.
2½"	1 yd.	2⅛ yds.	3¼ yds.
Fabric D (assorted prints for stars)			
Note: Amounts shown are generous totals.			
2"	½ yd.	1 yd.	1½ yds.
2½"	½ yd.	1 yd.	2 yds.
Border (red-and-blue stripe)			
2"	1½ yds.	1⅞ yds.	2¼ yds.
2½"	1¾ yds.	2⅜ yds.	3 yds.
Binding			
2"	⅝ yd.	¾ yd.	⅞ yd.
2½"	¾ yd.	⅞ yd.	1 yd.
Backing			
2"	1½ yds.	4 yds.	4¾ yds.
2½"	2 yds.	5 yds.	6 yds.
Batting			
2"	40" x 55"	55" x 70"	70" x 85"
2½"	47" x 67"	67" x 87"	87" x 108"

Cutting the Strips for Strip Sets, Blocks, and Borders

Refer to the cutting charts below and on page 45. Cut the required number of strips in the appropriate width to make the quilt size you have chosen. Cut all strips across the full width of the fabric (selvage to selvage) unless directed otherwise. All cut measurements include ¼"-wide seam allowances. Numbers in parentheses indicate how many full strips to cut in half for half-length strip sets. Refer to "Cutting Straight Strips" (page 7) for additional guidance as needed.

NUMBER OF STRIPS FOR STRIP SETS

FABRIC	STRIP WIDTH	*NUMBER OF STRIPS*		
		3 x 5 BLOCKS	5 x 7 BLOCKS	7 x 9 BLOCKS
A	2"	5 (1)	9	16 (3)
	2½"	5 (1)	12 (3)	18
B	2"	8 (1)	16	29 (4)
	2½"	8 (1)	21 (5)	32
C	2"	2 (1)	4	8 (1)
	2½"	2 (1)	6 (2)	8

NUMBER AND WIDTH OF ADDITIONAL FABRIC C STRIPS

This project requires additional fabric C strips cut in several different widths. Locate your chosen strip width in the chart (2" or 2½"); then cut the required number of C strips listed. Label these strips by letter (C1, C2) as you cut them.

STRIP WIDTH USED	WIDTH OF ADDITIONAL FABRIC C STRIPS	*NUMBER OF STRIPS*		
		3 x 5 BLOCKS	5 x 7 BLOCKS	7 x 9 BLOCKS
2"	1⅝"—C1*	4	8	15
	5"—C2	1	2	4 (1)
2½"	2"—C1*	5	11	19
	6½"—C2	1	3 (1)	4

*Set aside for Star blocks.

NUMBER OF BORDER STRIPS

Cut the borders along the length of the fabric.

FABRIC	STRIP WIDTH USED	*NUMBER OF 5½"-WIDE BORDER STRIPS*		
		3 x 5 BLOCKS	5 x 7 BLOCKS	7 x 9 BLOCKS
Red-and-blue stripe	2"	4	4	4
	2½"	4	4	4

Making the Strip Sets

Refer to the strip set diagrams above right and sew the appropriately sized and colored strips into strip sets. The strip set chart indicates the required number of each strip set for the quilt size you are making. Press seams in odd-numbered sets toward the last strip in the set. Press seams

in even-numbered sets toward the first strip in the set. Refer to "Making Strip Sets" (page 8) as needed.

Strip Set 1   Strip Set 2

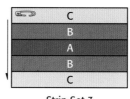

Strip Set 3   Strip Set 4

NUMBER OF STRIP SETS

STRIP SET NUMBER	STRIP WIDTH USED	*NUMBER OF STRIP SETS*		
		3 x 5 BLOCKS	5 x 7 BLOCKS	7 x 9 BLOCKS
1	2"	1	2	3, ½
	2½"	1	2, ½	4
2	2"	1	2	3, ½
	2½"	1	2, ½	4
3	2"	½	1	2
	2½"	½	1, ½	2
4	2"	1	2	3, ½
	2½"	1	2, ½	4

Each strip set 4 is made from 2 remaining strips of fabric B and 1 fabric C2 strip. These strip sets are used to make the Star blocks.

Cutting the Segments

Refer to the segment chart below to crosscut strip sets into the required number of segments for the quilt size you are making. Cut the segments to the same width as the individual strips in the strip sets. For example, if you are working with 2"-wide strips, cut the segments 2" wide from the strip set. Keep track of the cut segments from each strip set, always placing them so the first fabric in the segment is at the top. Refer to "Crosscutting Strip

Sets" (page 10) for guidance as needed. Note that the number of segments to cut in the segment chart is for both strip widths.

NUMBER OF SEGMENTS

STRIP SET NUMBER	NUMBER OF SEGMENTS		
	3 x 5 BLOCKS	5 x 7 BLOCKS	7 x 9 BLOCKS
1	16	36	64
2	16	36	64
3	8	18	32
4	14	34	62

Chain Block Construction

Refer to the block diagram at right to sew the segments into the appropriate number of Chain blocks. Press seams toward the center of the blocks. Mark the top left corner of each block with a safety pin. Refer to "Sewing the Blocks" (page 11) for guidance as needed.

Strip Set No.: 1 2 3 2 1

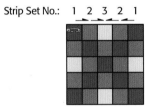

Chain Block
Make 8 for 3 x 5 block quilt.
Make 18 for 5 x 7 block quilt.
Make 32 for 7 x 9 block quilt.

Star Block Construction

Refer to the following cutting charts to prepare pieces for the Star blocks. Then follow steps 1 through 8 to make each Star block.

NUMBER AND SIZE OF FABRIC C1 PIECES

Cut fabric C1 strips into the appropriate number and size of rectangles and squares for the quilt size you are making.

STRIP WIDTH USED	PIECE SIZE	NUMBER OF PIECES		
		3 x 5 BLOCKS	5 x 7 BLOCKS	7 x 9 BLOCKS
2"	1⅝" x 2¾"	28	68	124
	1⅝" x 1⅝"	28	68	124
2½"	2" x 3½"	28	68	124
	2" x 2"	28	68	124

NUMBER AND SIZE OF FABRIC C3 PIECES

From the remaining fabric C, cut the following pieces. Label these pieces C3.

STRIP WIDTH USED	PIECE SIZE	NUMBER OF PIECES		
		3 x 5 BLOCKS	5 x 7 BLOCKS	7 x 9 BLOCKS
2"	2" x 5"	14	34	62
2½"	2½" x 6½"	14	34	62

NUMBER AND SIZE OF FABRIC D SQUARES FOR STAR BLOCKS

You'll need 7 Star blocks for a quilt with 3 x 5 blocks, 17 Star blocks for a quilt with 5 x 7 blocks, and 31 Star blocks for a quilt with 7 x 9 blocks. For each Star block, cut the following pieces from the same D fabric:

STRIP WIDTH USED	SMALL SQUARES		LARGE SQUARES	
	SIZE	NUMBER	SIZE	NUMBER
2"	1⅝" x 1⅝"	8	2¾" x 2¾"	1
2½"	2" x 2"	8	3½" x 3½"	1

1. Draw a diagonal line on the wrong side of each fabric D small square.
2. Place a marked square from step 1 with a fabric C1 rectangle, right sides together and raw edges aligned as shown. Stitch directly on the drawn line and trim away the excess, leaving a ¼" seam allowance. Press triangle toward the corner.

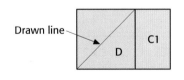

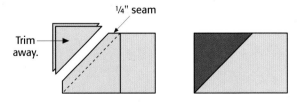

3. Sew a marked square from step 1 to the opposite side of the unit from step 2; trim and press. Make 4 units.

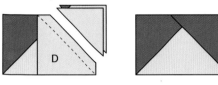

Star Point Unit

4. Sew a large fabric D square between 2 units from step 3 as shown. Press seams toward the large fabric D square.
5. Sew a remaining unit from step 3 between 2 fabric C1 squares as shown. Press the seams toward the fabric C1 squares. Make 2.
6. Sew the unit from step 4 between the units from step 5 as shown; press.

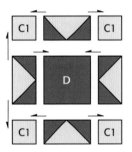

7. Sew a fabric C3 piece to the top and bottom of each star block. Press seams toward the fabric C3 piece.
8. Sew the unit from step 7 between 2 segments from strip set 4. Press seams toward the segments.

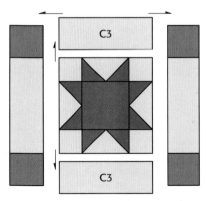

Make 7 for 3 x 5 block quilt.
Make 17 for 5 x 7 block quilt.
Make 31 for 7 x 9 block quilt.

Assembling the Quilt Top

1. Refer to the quilt diagram below to arrange alternating Chain and Star blocks. Sew the blocks together in horizontal rows. Press seams toward the Chain blocks.
2. Carefully pin the rows together to match the seams; then sew the rows together. Press the seams toward the bottom edge of the quilt.

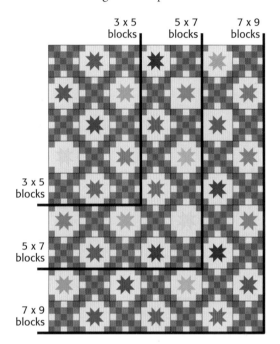

Quilt Diagram

Adding Borders

Refer to "Mitered Borders" (page 13) as needed to add the 5½"-wide red-and-blue striped border strips to the sides, top, and bottom of the quilt. Miter the corners; press.

Finishing

Refer to "Layering and Basting" (page 14), "Quilting" (page 14), and "Binding" (page 14) as needed.

1. Piece the quilt backing if necessary. Center the quilt top and batting over the backing; baste.
2. Quilt as desired.
3. Trim the backing and batting. Cut the binding fabric into 2½"-wide bias strips. Sew the binding to the quilt.

Bibliography

Carlson, Elizabeth Hamby. *Small Wonders: Tiny Treasures in Patchwork and Appliqué.* Woodinville, Washington: Martingale & Company, 1999.

Dietrich, Mimi. *Happy Endings: Finishing the Edges of Your Quilt.* Bothell, Washington: That Patchwork Place, 1987.

Hanson, Joan, and Mary Hickey. *The Joy of Quilting.* Bothell, Washington: That Patchwork Place, 1995.

Hargrave, Harriet, and Sharyn Craig. *The Art of Classic Quiltmaking.* Lafayette, California: C&T Publishing, 2000.

Spingola, Deanna. *Strip-Pieced Watercolor Magic.* Bothell, Washington: That Patchwork Place, 1996.

About the Author

Since making her first quilt in 1978, Elizabeth Hamby Carlson has made more quilts than she can count, and always has at least a dozen more in the planning stages. She began teaching quiltmaking in 1983 and especially enjoys sharing her methods for hand appliqué, machine piecing, and miniature quiltmaking with new quilters. She is the author of *Small Wonders: Tiny Treasures in Patchwork and Appliqué* (Martingale & Company, 1999). Through her pattern business, Elizabeth Quilts, she markets original quilt patterns that reflect her interest in the decorative arts and quilting traditions of the eighteenth and nineteenth centuries. In addition to her traditional quilts, Elizabeth, a lifelong Anglophile, also designs and makes quilts inspired by her interest in English history. Her award-winning quilts have been featured in numerous quilt publications and have been exhibited across the United States and England.

Raised in northeastern Ohio, Elizabeth now lives with her husband in Montgomery Village, Maryland. She has a grown son and daughter, each of whom has lots of quilts. When Elizabeth is not quilting, she enjoys reading, antiquing, and planning her next trip to England.